Manga Drawing Books How to Draw Manga Female Face (B/W)

Learn Japanese Manga Eyes and Pretty Manga Face

By Gala Publication

PUBLISHED BY:

Gala Publication

ISBN-13: 978- 1508697121
ISBN-10: 1508697124

©Copyright 2015 – Gala Publication

By Gala Publication

Table Of Content :

Manga-style-female faces 1

Step 1

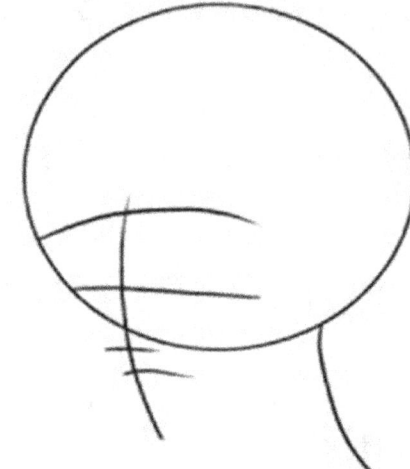

Step 2

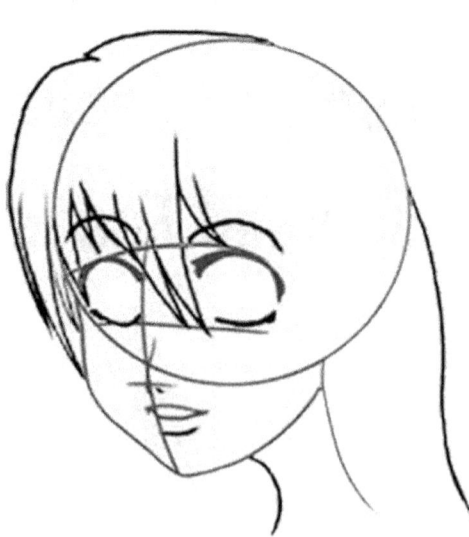

Step 3

Step 4

Step 5

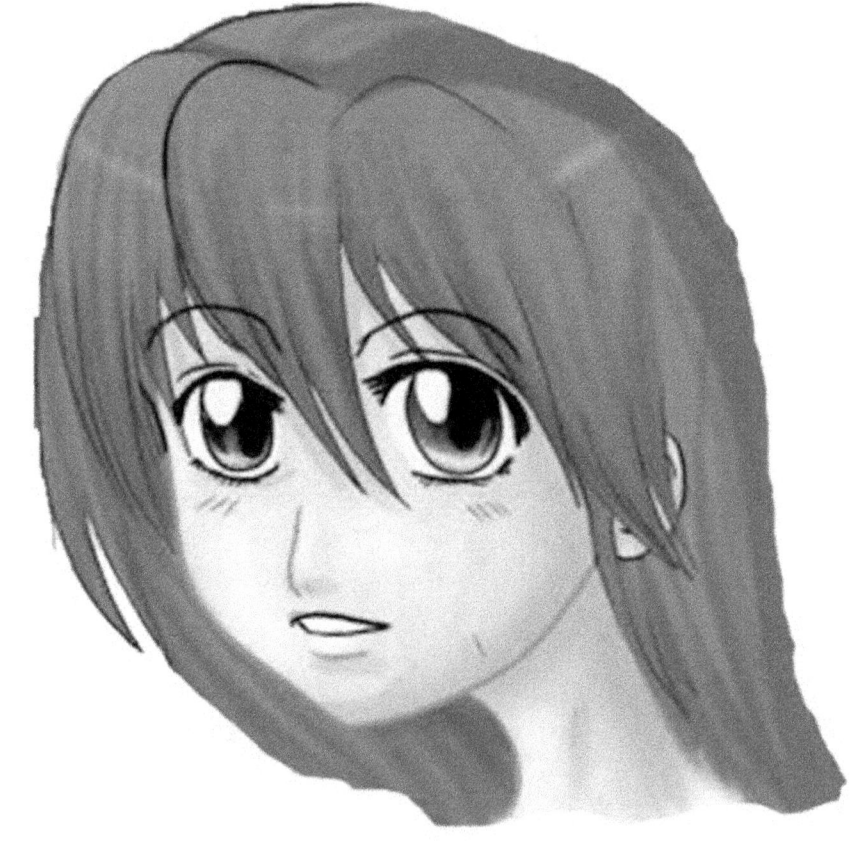

Manga style female faces 2

Step 1

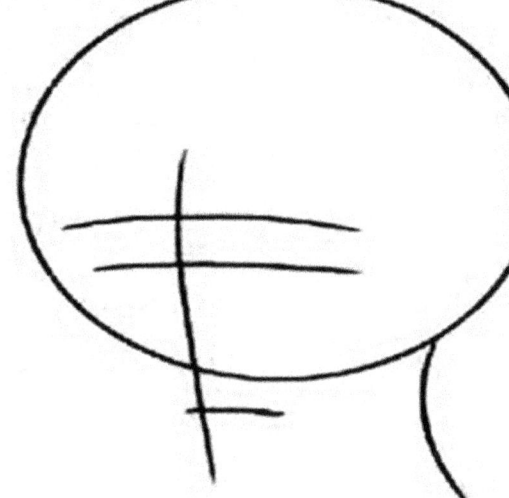

Step 2

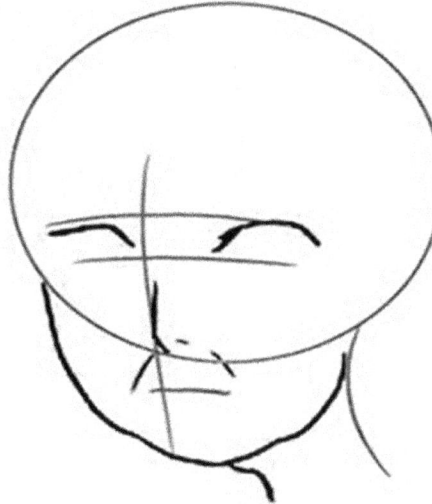

Step 3

Step 4

Step 5

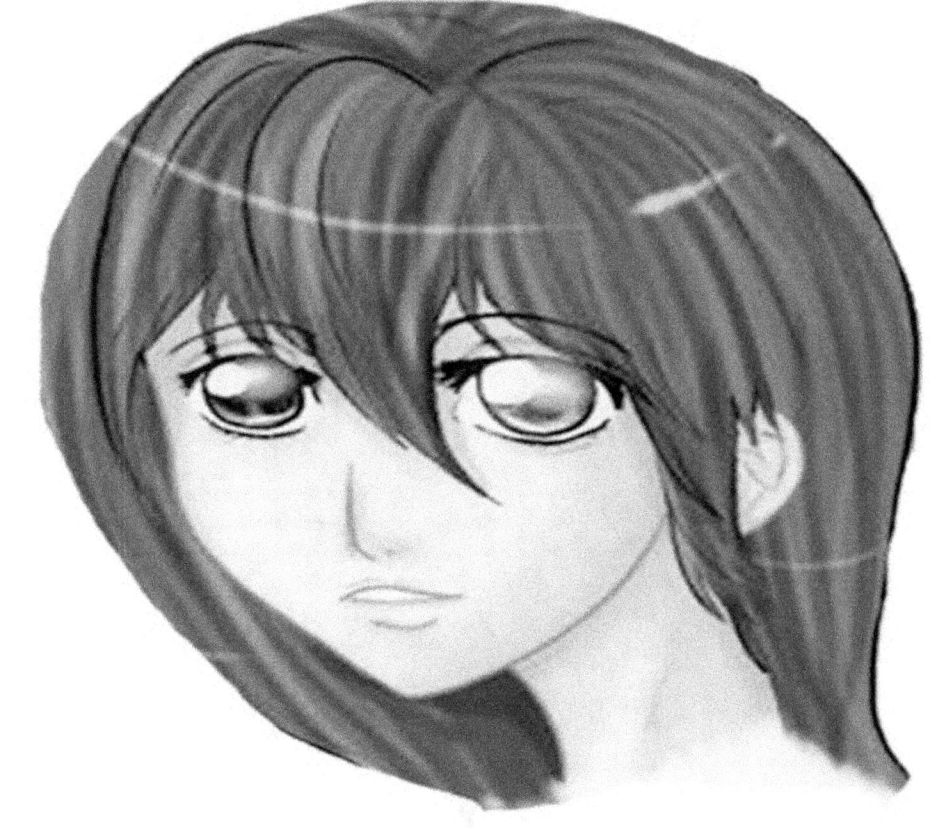

Manga style female faces 3

Step 1

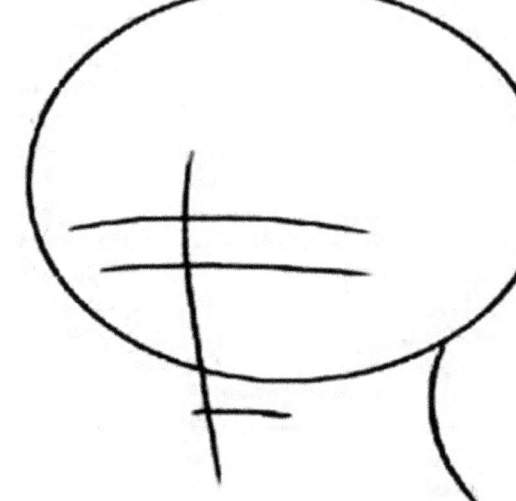

Step 2

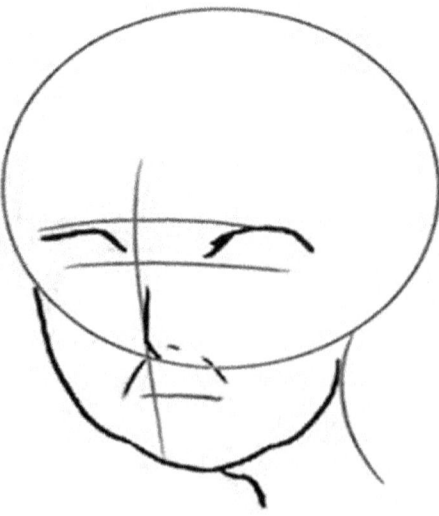

Step 3

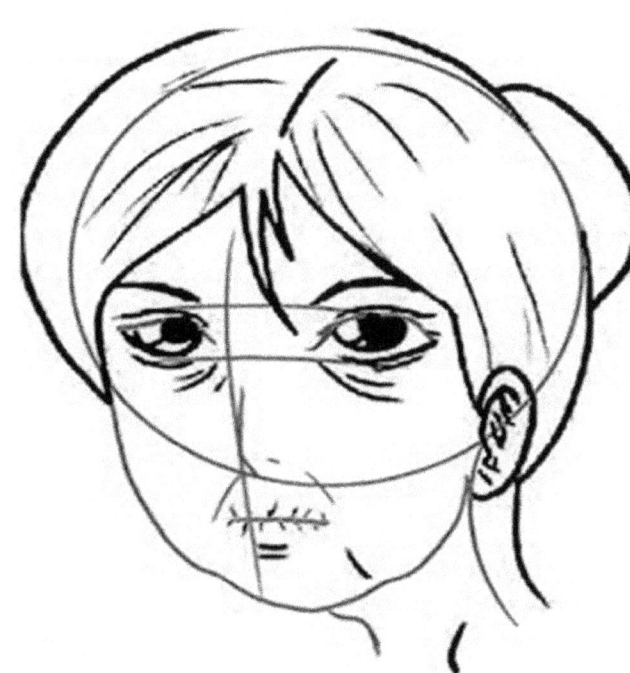

Step 4

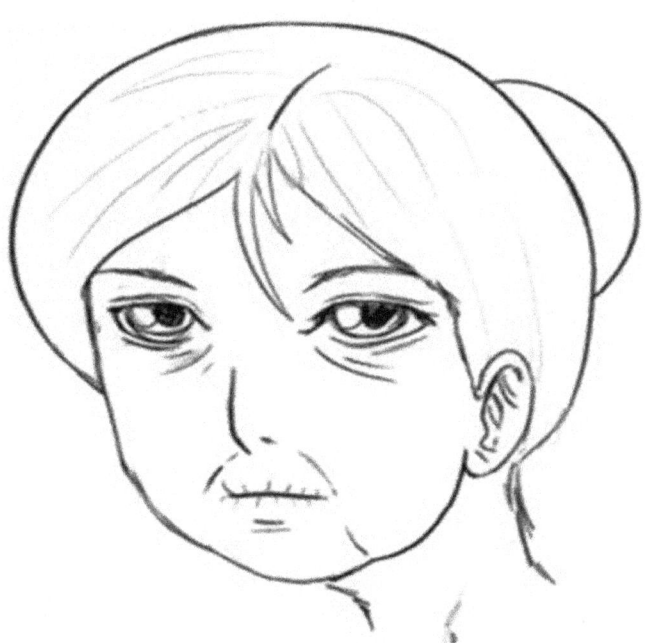

Step 5

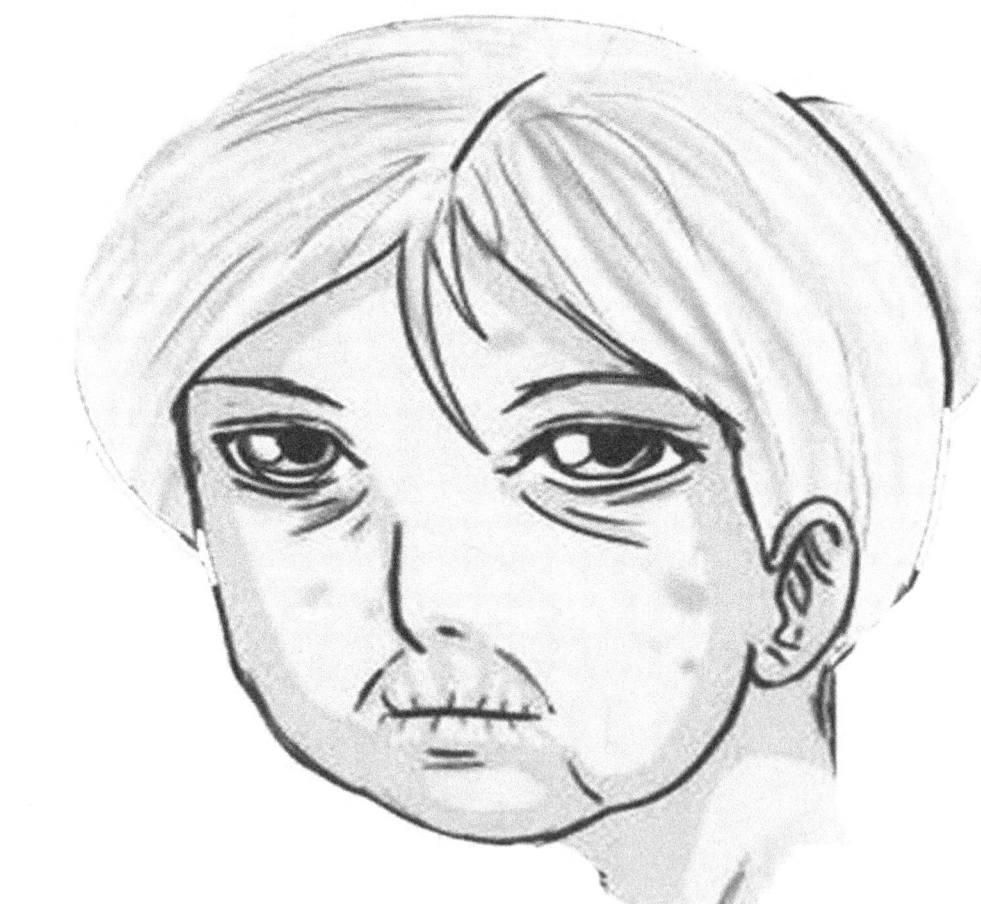

Manga style female faces 4

Step 1

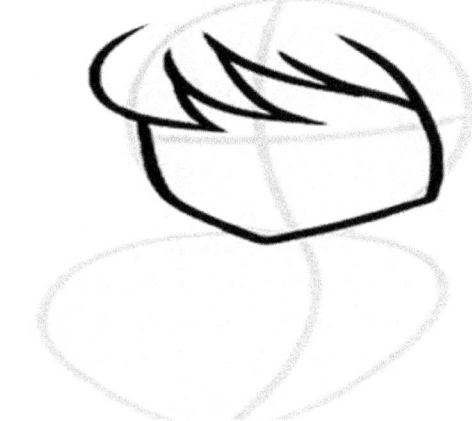

Step 2

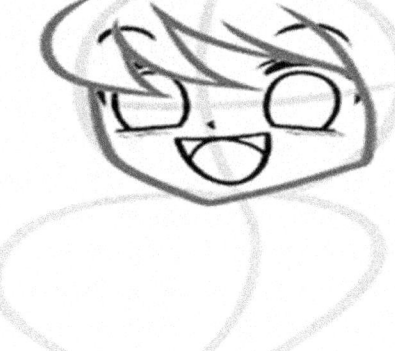

Step 3

Step 4

Step 5

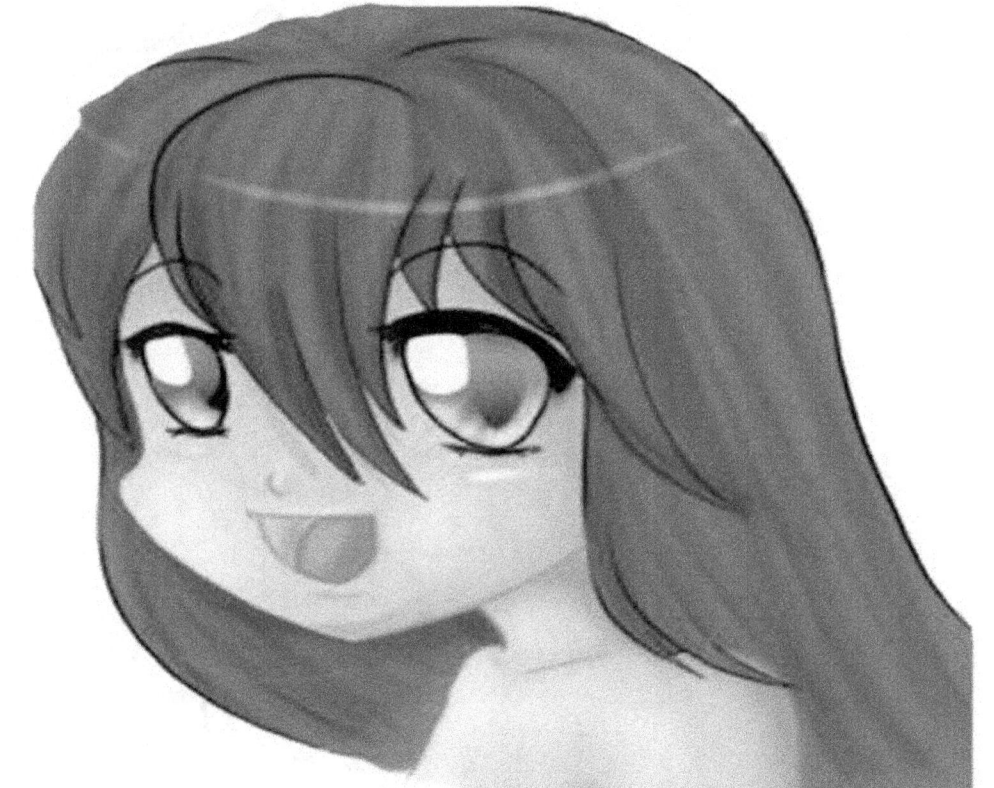

Manga style female faces 5

Step 1

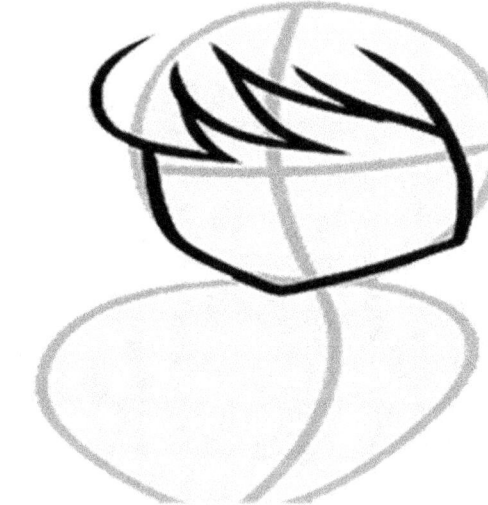

Step 2

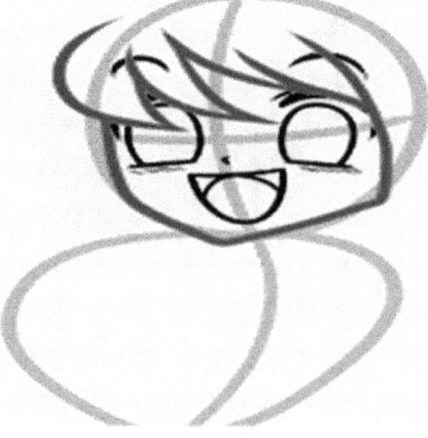

Step 3

Step 4

Step 5

Step 6

Step 7

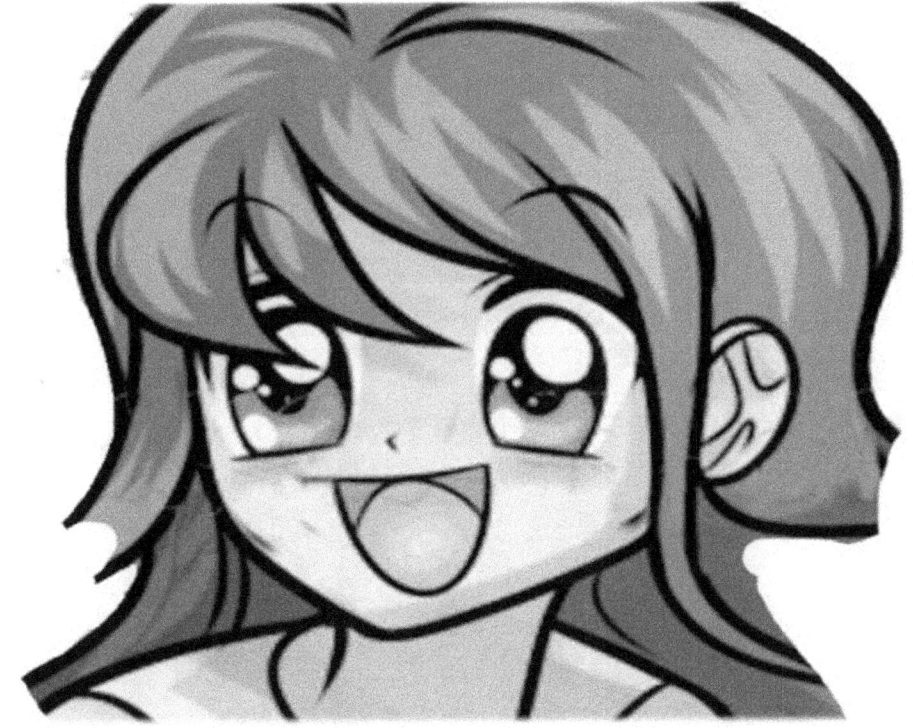

Surprised face 1

Step 1

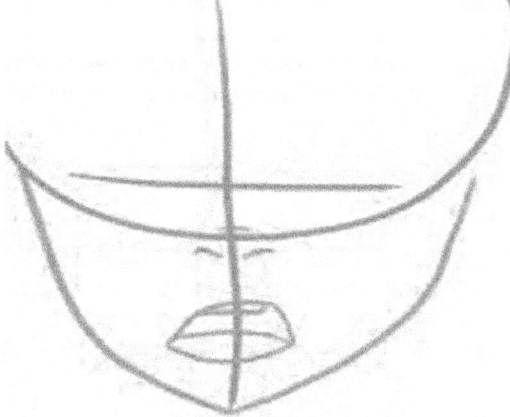

Step 2

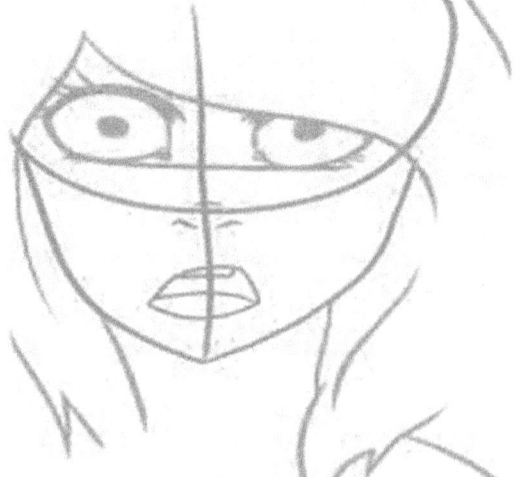

Step 3

Step 4

Step 5

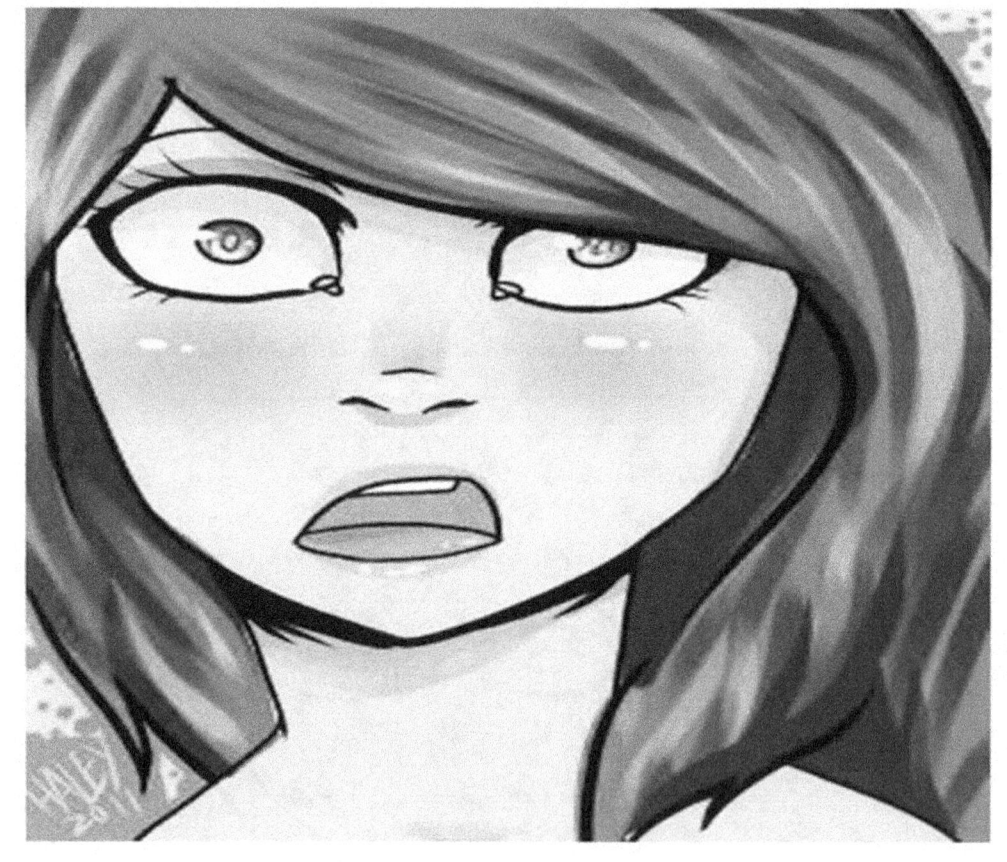

Surprised face 2

Step 1

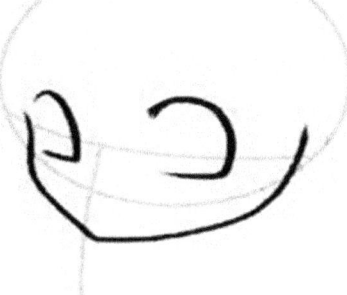

Step 2

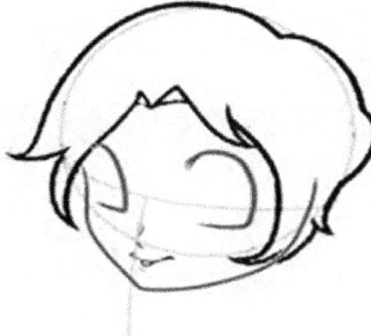

Step 3

Step 4

Step 5

Step 6

Step 7

THE END

www.ingramcontent.com/pod-product-compliance
Lightning Source LLC
Chambersburg PA
CBHW080628180526
45168CB00007B/3090